The ATTORNEY'S GUIDE *to Using (or Not Using)* LEGAL RECRUITERS

Answers to important questions most attorneys don't know to ask ... but should

DAN BINSTOCK

The Attorney's Guide to Using (or Not Using) Legal Recruiters
Answers to important questions most attorneys don't know to ask ... but should

Dan Binstock

ISBN: 978-0-692-60321-5

To the many attorneys who have entrusted me with their lateral moves during such an important time in their careers. Thank you.

PRAISE FOR "THE ATTORNEY'S GUIDE TO USING (OR NOT USING) LEGAL RECRUITERS"

Dan is known across North America as one of the smartest, most honest voices in the recruitment industry today, and this book captures his essence perfectly – a great, insightful, and honest account of how the legal recruiter industry works and what you need to know about working with a recruiter.

WARREN SMITH, ESQ.
MANAGING PARTNER, THE COUNSEL NETWORK
PRESIDENT, NATIONAL ASSOCIATION OF LEGAL SEARCH CONSULTANTS (NALSC)

Good recruiters leverage their vast network and help attorneys navigate the recruiting process. Great recruiters bring a discipline and honesty to the attorney's job search that will significantly increase the likelihood of finding the "right fit" for both the attorney and their new employer. Dan is master of this art; he further takes attorneys from feeling like they are on a precipice to a safe and confident place during this life-changing decision making process. This Guide empowers attorneys to make an informed and tailored decision if they need such a shepherd.

ADRIENNE PRENTICE, ESQ.
DIRECTOR & ASSOCIATE GENERAL COUNSEL, HEWLETT PACKARD ENTERPRISE

If you are a partner or associate considering using a legal recruiter, this Guide helps to demystify the process. Aligning with the right recruiter is a significant decision and can impact your lateral move on various levels. The more educated you are on your options and the different moving pieces, the better.

ANAND DAVID
GLOBAL DIRECTOR, LATERAL PARTNER RECRUITING, WHITE & CASE LLP

Lateral recruiting, particularly on the partner level, is very complex. Lawyers entering the lateral market should know that a lack of understanding about the intricacies of the process will invariably lead to issues which can adversely affect their candidacies. Along with education, a skilled legal recruiter can make a world of difference in making the process run smoothly for both the candidate and the law firm.

Mieko Rechka
Senior Manager of Partner Recruiting, Sidley Austin, LLP

If you are a lawyer who is thinking of changing jobs, don't do so until you read this book. Dan demystifies the process of using a recruiter by shining a bright light on what were — until now — the secrets of the trade. Armed with Dan's incredible knowledge and wisdom as a tenured, top recruiter, you will be better equipped to find and land the career of your dreams after reading this book.

Caryn Ulrich Stacy
CEO, Diversity Lab and On-Ramp Fellowship
Adjunct Professor, University of Denver Sturm College of Law
Managing Editor, TalentThinkTank.com

This Guide is a much-needed resource for candidates considering a lateral move. In my role as a hiring partner, I am surprised when strong candidates allow weaker recruiters to represent them, which can create challenges during the process. Reading this Guide will enable you to make smarter decisions regarding your recruiter.

Shon Glusky, Esq.
Co-Practice Group Leader, Corporate Practice, Sheppard, Mullin, Richter & Hampton, LLP
Co-Chair, Lateral Partner Recruiting for New York office

Dan Binstock provides insight and valuable counsel on every page. If you are entertaining the idea of a move, you need to read this work. He addresses not only the fundamentals of a move, but the consideration of candidates first, and all of the oft missed elements of statutory, case, and ethics requirements so that the relocation is done right, for which so many others have no clue. If you are thinking of a move, read this.

Edwin Reeser, Esq.
Renowned Legal Industry Consultant and President of Edwin B. Reeser, A Professional Law Corporation
Fmr. Managing Partner of Sonnenschein's Los Angeles Office

There's a reason I invite Dan to speak to my Georgetown Law students each year: in addition to being an expert on the DC legal market, he presents insider information in a clear and comprehensive way, without bias or agenda. With this Guide, Dan provides a similar service to attorneys facing the strategic decisions and administrative challenges that accompany a career shift. Simply put, it just makes sense for an attorney considering a lateral move to use this (highly readable!) Guide before beginning the process.

Robert Cacace, Esq.
Associate Director, Georgetown Law Office of Career Services

Dan Binstock's Guide provides attorney job-seekers essential inside intelligence on when, how, and why to use (or not use) recruiters. Well-written and accessible, the Guide reveals the thought processes of legal search consultants and prospective employers, and shows readers how to use that information to boost their chances of getting hired.

Valerie Fontaine, Esq.
Partner, Selzer Fontaine Beckwith
Author of "The Right Moves: Job Search and Career Development Strategies for Lawyers"

The process of using a legal recruiter involves much more than meets the eye. Unless you are an insider, you can't know the various dynamics and nuances. This Guide should be required reading for any attorney working with a recruiter, as it could save you from making costly missteps.

Teresa Bernstein, Esq.
Chief Legal Officer/Chief Compliance Officer, ACON Investments

CONTENTS

SECTION I: WORKING WITH LEGAL RECRUITERS

ABOUT THE GUIDE

Legal recruiters can play an important role in the careers of attorneys, but there is surprisingly little information available regarding the process of selecting and engaging a recruiter and best protecting your interests. For example, when should you use a recruiter versus applying to a position on your own? What types of employers do and don't use recruiters? What type of information will the recruiter keep confidential versus having a duty to disclose to the employer? How do you determine whether the smooth and confident phone demeanor of a cold caller is rooted in actual substantive knowledge, or whether you are simply hearing well-rehearsed buzzwords? Most importantly, what steps can you take to ensure the maximum level of insight, guidance, and confidentiality during your search process? Yes, you have a level of control over these things.

This Guide—focused on major legal markets in the United States—will provide you with an insider's perspective into these and other important questions. While targeted more toward attorneys who are new to working with recruiters, this Guide will contain practical tips and advice applicable to attorneys at all levels — from junior associates to seasoned partners — who wish to gain more insight into the process. Whether you choose to read this from beginning to end or only reference particular sections, you will walk away more knowledgeable about how recruiters may (or may not) fit into your search, how best to respond to calls and emails, and how to avoid the most common missteps.

Special thanks to my colleague and partner, Martha Ann Sisson, for her valuable insights on this Guide.

First Edition, November 2015

AUTHOR

Dan Binstock is a partner of Garrison & Sisson, an attorney search firm based in Washington, DC since 1986 and consistently voted "Best Legal Recruiting Firm" in DC by the National Law Journal/Legal Times. Garrison & Sisson focuses on placing partners and associates in a wide range of prominent law firms and in-house legal departments. Dan currently serves as the Chair of the Ethics Committee for the National Association of Legal Search Consultants (NALSC).

Dan is considered an authority on the lateral attorney market and has led presentations at industry conferences and law schools around the country. Dan's commentary on the legal market has appeared in the media including The Wall Street Journal, The Washington Post, The National Law Journal/Legal Times, Law360, Washington Business Journal, Bloomberg/BNA, Fortune, The Boston Globe, ABA Journal, The American Lawyer, The Legal Intelligencer, Above the Law, Washingtonian, and Bisnow Legal, among others.

Prior to becoming a legal recruiter in 2004, Dan practiced intellectual property law with Finnegan Henderson, a prominent intellectual property boutique. He earned his J.D., *magna cum laude*, from Washington College of Law and his undergraduate degree in psychology from the University of Maryland during which time he also performed as the pianist for the musical political comedy troupe, the Capitol Steps.

SECTION I

THE TRUTH ABOUT LEGAL RECRUITERS

CHAPTER 1

THE BASICS: WHAT RECRUITERS DO, WHY THEY EXIST, AND WHO PAYS THEM

RECRUITERS SERVE TWO PRIMARY FUNCTIONS AND HAVE TWO MASTERS

Function 1: Help attorneys locate and obtain the most suitable career opportunities.

- Why attorneys use recruiters:
  - Gain access to the "invisible job market" (openings that never become public or recruiter-only searches)
  - Provide insider knowledge (good and bad) on the market
  - Assist with resume, deal sheets, business plans, etc.
  - Ensure confidentiality
  - Delegate the time and legwork associated with a job search
  - Recruiter's "relationship factor" and personal endorsement can inure to your benefit
  - Gain an advocate to help navigate the moving pieces of the process (understanding the norms, interview preparation, negotiating offers)

Function 2: Help employers find the most suitable attorney for their job.

- Why employers hire recruiters:
  - Gain access to high-quality passive candidates who are not otherwise searching for a job
  - Save time by avoiding the legwork of researching, contacting, and engaging with potential candidates
  - Recruiters screen and present the most qualified candidates
  - Recruiters are able to interview for cultural fit and shared objectives
  - Receive guidance during the interview/candidate selection and offer processes
  - Gain knowledge about the market and the firm's place in it (in a way that is not otherwise readily available)

WHO PAYS?

The employer. There is no cost to the attorney who is being placed. The recruiter is only compensated if and when you are placed and remain employed for a certain amount of time. The employer pays the placement fee, which is negotiated in advance of your referral.

ECONOMIC JUSTIFICATION

Minimal training: When employers pay recruiters, they are paying for the experience and training the attorney received from another employer. This ability to hire an attorney who can "hit the ground running" can save the hiring firm a significant amount of money, training, and risk.

Higher quality candidate/likelihood of long-term success: Nobody likes paying for something if they don't have to, and that includes paying for recruiters. Indeed, some firms will offer financial incentives to their own attorneys to refer their contacts for current openings at their own firm. This provides a relationship-vetted endorsement and may lower the cost associated with recruiting the individual. That said, the primary reason employers engage a search firm includes access to a higher quality applicant pool and assistance in navigating the process. According to feedback we have received from Hiring Managers at AmLaw 100 firms who track statistics for lateral hiring, candidates referred by search firms tend to be of a higher quality and more successful in the long-term than those who self-apply. As stated by one Manager, "Approximately 75% of our hires over the past three years came through recruiters. ...Our partners understand that laterals referred by recruiters are usually stronger candidates because they are not necessarily looking for a job. The best candidates pay for themselves." Another commented, "Our partners want to hire attorneys who are in demand in their current firms and don't need a job. Recruiters are seen as the most effective way to access these attorneys."

WHY ARE RECRUITERS SELECTIVE?

Recruiters serve to remedy a market imbalance by providing attorneys to employers where there is a high demand but not enough supply. It's important to note that recruiters don't *want* to be selective — if it were up to recruiters, they would be able to work with and place all types of attorneys. The reality is that recruiters (who focus on permanent placements as opposed to temporary or contract placements) are unable to work with a vast majority of the attorney population. In my personal experience, for every ten referrals I receive, I can assist fewer than three of those attorneys. This is because the types of employers who use recruiters have specific requirements in terms of academic pedigree and relevant experience.

Because recruiters work on contingency, they can only present candidates who match the hiring criteria of employers.

BOTTOM LINE — DO NOT TAKE IT PERSONALLY

If you contact a few recruiters and none are able to assist you, do not interpret this as meaning you are unemployable. If not volunteered by your recruiter, inquire why they are unable to assist you. The supply and demand of the market determines what a recruiter can and cannot do. And, it may mean that applying to employers directly is a more appropriate strategy for you. Attorneys with backgrounds consistent with AmLaw 100 firms and their hiring criteria are in greatest demand.

CHAPTER 2

EMPLOYERS WHO USE RECRUITERS AND THOSE WHO DON'T

Using a recruiter is a luxury for employers, but not all employers seek to invest in recruiters (the market rate for search firm fees is approximately 25% of the hired attorney's first-year compensation). The following is an overview of which employer types tend to use legal recruiters and which do not.

EMPLOYERS WHO TEND TO USE RECRUITERS

- **Larger law firms (AmLaw 100/200).** Because large firms tend to charge the highest rates, their clients are the most demanding in terms of the quality of the attorneys and work product. These firms appreciate that the highest (or higher) caliber attorneys are required to attract and maintain high-quality clients. They realize that recruiters provide the fastest access to the most accomplished and best-vetted attorneys in the market (including those who are not actively looking for a job). Accordingly, they budget for recruiting fees.
- **Higher-end boutiques, such as specialty boutiques or spin-offs from larger firms.** High-end boutiques tend to share a similar client base and the same recruiting philosophies as larger firms. While their billing rates may be more flexible, they also want access to the best attorneys in the market to maintain their high-end clients. Also, some do not have formal summer associate programs so

they may prefer to hire more experienced attorneys who have been trained by another employer and can immediately begin contributing to the bottom line.

- **Corporations/in-house legal departments**. In-house legal departments hire attorneys who match numerous requirements that go far beyond what is simply on a resume. To make the right match requires not only the right legal skill set and background, but appropriate business and interpersonal skills that mesh with the company's culture. This is very difficult to screen for on a resume, so recruiters play a valuable role in sourcing, vetting, and presenting the short list of the most appropriate candidates for the employer to consider.
- **Associations** (e.g., trade associations). Same rationale as corporations/in-house legal departments discussed above.

EMPLOYERS WHO TEND NOT TO USE RECRUITERS

- Government agencies (hiring is handled internally)
- Non-profits/public interest
- Smaller/local law firms (e.g., those with a less commercial client base, including plaintiff/personal injury firms, criminal (non-white collar) defense, insurance defense, family law, estate planning, workers compensation, etc.)
- Some larger firms, including those handling commoditized work and generally paying below market

In addition to the financial cost associated with the use of a legal recruiter, other factors influencing this decision include:

- Supply vs. demand for the particular profile (discussed later)
- The urgency of the need
- The importance the employer places on finding "the best person" versus "the best person seeking a job right now"
- Whether the employer has an internal legal recruiting department and its level of resources and skill

CHAPTER 3

BACKGROUNDS *NOT* SUITED TO WORKING WITH A RECRUITER

DO NOT USE A RECRUITER IF

- You are seeking an **entry-level position** (either a recent law school or LL.M. graduate). Most employers have processes in place for hiring entry-level attorneys, such as on-campus recruiting. Recent graduates don't yet have the experience that employers will require of candidates referred through a recruiter.
- You are applying to **government or non-profit positions**. Most government and non-profit agencies don't have budgets for external recruiters.
- You are interested in an employer that **doesn't use recruiters** or the website job posting states "no recruiters."

  Sometimes there are exceptions to the "no recruiters/principals only" notice on a website. Here's why: When a law firm posts a position, numerous recruiters around the country become aware of the position through various website monitoring tools and may begin calling candidates, even if the recruiter does not have a relationship with the employer or knowledge about the position. This may not reflect well on the employer for a variety of reasons. Some firms try to curtail unfamiliar recruiters from working on their searches by posting "no recruiters/principals only" but will contact their one or two "go-to" recruiters for assistance.

BE CAREFUL WORKING WITH A RECRUITER IF

- You will be searching for a position **after a clerkship (and you do not have prior practice experience)**. In most major legal markets, firms view post-judicial clerks as entry-level hires despite your excellent clerkship experience. A number of our clients have explicit language in their agreements prohibiting the referral and placement of clerks who do not have prior practice experience. **Possible exceptions**:

  - You are interested in a smaller metropolitan area that does not routinely attract attorneys with federal clerkships. Some firms in these legal communities will pay recruiters for access to these candidates. **Tip**: If a recruiter wishes to present you to a firm, ask: (1) if they are authorized to present candidates who have just completed a judicial clerkship to the firm, and (2) have they ever placed a judicial clerk at the particular firm?
  - You have relevant industry experience **as an attorney** prior to your clerkship. In these circumstances, some firms will view you as a lateral given your practice experience. This depends, of course, on several moving pieces such as your practice area, academic background, and the firm's level of need.

- You are a junior associate with:

  - Non-AmLaw 100 firm pedigree including law school attended and/or class rank
  - Experience is **not** from an AmLaw 200 firm or high-end boutique

- You are a senior associate in a practice area that is saturated with available talent in the market (e.g., litigation), and there is little turnover or demand.

- You are in a practice area that may function as a service type of practice area (e.g., trusts and estates, certain types of labor and employment law experience) at most firms, with little lateral demand.
- You are a Partner or Counsel without portable business and/or a track record of attracting and retaining clients.
- **You have been asked to leave your firm.**
  - **Duty to disclose**: Even though ethical recruiters will treat information you share with them in confidence, the interests of the employers must be considered. (This is discussed in detail later in the Guide.) Employers expect recruiters to disclose information about a candidate that would be "material to the hiring decision." Frequently such a requirement is included in the fee agreement between the employer and the recruiting firm. When it comes to being laid off (even if you are still on the firm's website, receiving healthcare benefits, and technically employed), potential employers consider the pending non-self-initiated departure from an employer to be a material fact. If your departure is unrelated to performance issues, a recruiter may be positioned to, and can, advise you on communicating the circumstances to a future employer with integrity and in a manner that prevents (or minimizes) the employer from making negative assumptions. If you wish to obfuscate the motivation for your pending departure, think carefully about using a recruiter.

  Having seen these situations play out many different ways over the years, I believe that honesty coupled with a thoughtful explanation as to the circumstances surrounding your departure is the best policy. Lawyers on the hiring side tend to sniff out situations that "don't add up," and the cover up is always worse than the crime. There's no recovery if caught in a fabrication. In short — don't do it.

SHORTHAND TEST

Here's a shorthand test to determine whether you might want to consider working with a recruiter. If you find yourself pursuing recruiters (i.e., applying to their postings or calling them) but are not getting a response; or you're consistently getting the response of, "we'll keep your materials on file and let you know if anything comes up," this is probably a signal that recruiters don't believe your background is in high enough demand by their clients. If this is your experience, as mentioned previously, you are not alone. **The vast majority of the attorneys in the United States who reach out to recruiters experience this.**

Oftentimes, the attorneys best situated to use a recruiter are those who have been actively pursued by recruiters and already know they are in demand. That said, because you are pursued by a recruiter does not mean that the particular recruiter is best situated for you, as discussed later in this Guide.

CHAPTER 4

BACKGROUNDS SUITED TO WORKING WITH A RECRUITER

As mentioned previously, the decision for an attorney to work with a recruiter is driven by **supply and demand** in the market. This is a subjective and nuanced analysis. The more seasoned a recruiter, the more experienced he or she is at making this determination. Let's explore the backgrounds of attorneys best suited to using a recruiter.

ASSOCIATES SEEKING LAW FIRM POSITIONS

The sweet spot:

- Between two and five years of law firm work experience at an AmLaw 200 firm or high-end specialty boutique
- Strong academic pedigree (top 25 law school, or top 10-15% of the class in a non-top 25 school is preferred)
- Experience and training in an in-demand practice area
- Government experience directly transferable to law firm practice in the particular city

Recruiter's placeability analysis: Here's a list of the different factors a recruiter considers when evaluating whether he/she can affirmatively assist a candidate:

- Pedigree (law school, grades, etc.)
- Current employer (strength of current firm, perceived quality of training)
- Practice area (supply vs. demand)
- Level of experience (per above, most associate needs are for two to five years)
- Reason for considering a move (is it a voluntary departure or has the attorney been asked to leave the current employer?)
- Stability (number of job changes, tenure in positions, reasons for moves)
- Personality and cultural fit

ASSOCIATES SEEKING IN-HOUSE POSITIONS

As you likely know or will soon find out, in-house positions remain among the most sought after opportunities.

The sweet spot:

- Between four and eight years of law firm work experience at an AmLaw 200 firm or high-end specialty boutique
- Directly relevant experience as defined by the company for the in-house position
- Secondment to a client is a plus
- MBA or accounting degree, or other relevant Master's degree (e.g., Master of Public Health)

- Assuming role as de facto in-house counsel for some of your clients

Recruiter's placeability analysis:

- Current employer (strength of current firm, perceived quality of training)
- Practice area/type of experience
- Relevant client industry exposure, if any
- Years of experience in relevant area
- Your motivations for going in-house
- Pre-law school business experience
- Ability to demonstrate an understanding of business goals within acceptable legal risks
- Stability in current position and number of prior job changes
- Personality/cultural fit

PARTNERS SEEKING LAW FIRMS

For the individual seeking a position, the analysis undertaken by the potential employer includes:

- Practice area expertise
- Portable business (i.e., how much work can you bring with you), as well as your potential to generate business in the future. **Note**: For lateral partners, minimum portable business usually starts at $500,000. At the most profitable firms (e.g., those with profits-

per-partner over $2 million), the expectation can be a minimum of $2.5 to $5 million in portable business. **Exception**: the need is for a partner with a specific skill set to service existing clients and without this skill set, the firm may lose work. **Other exceptions**: (1) if the attorney is coming from a senior level appointed position in government or an in-house position that can translate into significant business development potential, and/or a reputation sufficient to "draw clients in;" or (2) the attorney is more junior (e.g., a senior associate or counsel) but has demonstrated business development potential.

Recruiter's placeability analysis:

- Practice area (how in demand is practice area?)
- Consistent record of stable, diverse and growing client relationships
- Level of "portable" business (how much business will likely move or be developed at the new firm within the next twelve months)
- Successful demonstration of cross-marketing your clients to others for their expertise
- Reasonable compensation expectations (how likely is it that a new firm will match or exceed the amount the partner is currently earning?)
- Billing rate
- Number of portable clients (in some instances, the more clients the better because it diversifies the sources of revenue)
- Types of clients (synergies, leveragability, and the industry sector they occupy)

- Reason for considering a move; prior number of moves
- Personality/cultural fit
- Ability to move with key team members

CHAPTER 5

SHOULD YOU USE A PERSONAL CONTACT INSTEAD OF A RECRUITER?

The short answer is "maybe." This question comes up often and making the right decision requires consideration of numerous factors.

Factors to consider:

- **Is your contact held in high regard**? This is perhaps the most important consideration. It is only human nature to view a referral and/or a reference as an extension of that personal contact's internal reputation. You may benefit or be penalized accordingly (even if on a subconscious level) in the eyes of the hiring individuals.

- **Does the contact know your narrative and the reasons for making a move, and can he/she present them effectively?**

  Your contact should be able to do more than simply forward a resume to the recruiting department with a quick note saying, "*This person is a friend from law school and is interested in our firm. Please consider. Thx.*" In a perfect world, your contact should provide context for your interest in being considered by the firm. For example, why are you considering a move? What are some of your relevant strengths, and why might you be a fit for the new firm?

- **Can the contact endorse you?**

- **Is the contact potentially threatened by you or could view you as competition?**

  The typical person wants to be helpful to his/her friends and contacts, and is happy to forward a resume and help someone get a foot in the door. It's a win/win if your affiliation with the new firm can serve to benefit your referring contact's career at the firm. But there's a flip side. What if your addition to the firm creates more competition for your personal contact? You may have relationships with the same contacts and potential clients, which could duplicate your contact's business development plans. You can see how this may turn out if you are viewed as a threat. Your referring contact may be in a position to exercise a heightened level of internal control over your candidacy, for better or worse.

- **Will the contact have a vested interest in your joining the firm and advocate for you?**

  Like any process with numerous moving pieces and people, things can slow down or come to a halt for any number of reasons. Sometimes the process stalls because the key decision makers are simply too busy to focus on the hire, or may have some reservations about your suitability. Regardless of the reason, your internal contact should have a vested interest in your joining and, just as importantly, be positioned to provide the appropriate types of gentle pushes (which can be handled in a variety of manners) if and when things get bottlenecked.

- **How much guidance would you like during the process?**

  If you have significant experience with the lateral process, you may feel comfortable with a "do it yourself" approach because you know what to expect. On the other hand, if you are the type of attorney who appreciates others' expertise, having a consultant provides perspective and market norms on the application process.

A recruiter will also make the process less administratively burdensome. Sending in your resume is similar to the first mile in a marathon.

And:

- **Are you comfortable negotiating compensation on your own behalf?**

  One of the more awkward aspects of the lateral process is negotiating with a person who could be a future colleague or partner. There's a fine line between advocating for yourself and obtaining your full market value versus pushing a bit too hard and turning off your future colleagues. If you are a good negotiator (including for yourself) and can "leave it on the field" when it's done, you will be fine so long as you are knowledgeable about your market value and know when enough is enough. But if negotiating regarding your own compensation makes you a bit uneasy—or you feel you might undervalue or over-value yourself—let your recruiter serve as the intermediary.

SIDEBAR: WHAT'S YOUR POSTURE? ARE YOU BEING POACHED OR JOB SEARCHING?

Employers place a premium on candidates who are perceived as being "poached" versus "looking for a job." When someone is being poached, employers tend to focus more on how they can provide a platform that better meets your needs and interests. The burden is on the employer and their competitive nature often tends to kick in. On the other hand, when someone is perceived as job searching, there may be more scrutiny on your candidacy. The employer needs to first clarify questions such as "Why is this person looking for a job?" or "Is there something we're missing?" This certainly does not mean that people who are looking for a job are branded as less qualified, but it's just a subtle difference in positioning and distinguishing yourself at the outset, thus affecting the tone and direction of discussions.

CHAPTER 6

WHAT IS REQUIRED TO BECOME A RECRUITER, WHY SHOULD YOU CARE, AND THE 9 RISKS ASSOCIATED WITH USING AN INEFFECTIVE RECRUITER

Legal recruiting is an unregulated industry with no bar to entry. Although an increasing number of legal recruiters are former practicing lawyers, there is no certification process to becoming or remaining a recruiter. There are two things required to becoming a legal recruiter: a computer and telephone. That's all. As a result, recruiters come in all shapes, sizes, and ethical fabrics.

Consider the below chart.

REQUIREMENTS	LAWYER	LEGAL RECRUITER
UNDERGRADUATE DEGREE	Yes	No
LAW DEGREE	Yes	No
LICENSURE	Yes	No
CHARACTER/ETHICAL FITNESS	Yes	No
ONGOING CLE REQUIREMENTS	Yes	No

What does this mean for you?

Unfortunately, you can't assume that a recruiter who calls you has any background, training, or knowledge of the legal industry or marketplace. Many experienced and ethical recruiters have your best interest in mind, but other bad apples are drawn to the idea of making "easy money" as explained below.

9 RISKS ASSOCIATED WITH USING AN INEFFECTIVE RECRUITER

Similar to lawyers handling contingency fee cases, recruiters earn a commission-based salary dependent on completed placements. They earn a fee if they place you and nothing if they don't. If a recruiter is driven solely by the pursuit of a fee and their self-serving financial interest in a particular transaction — rather than a desire to assist in making a good marriage between two parties — this recruiter is not grounded in a larger professional motivation with an emphasis on what is in the best interests of all parties. Without this larger motivation, the recruiter may be more likely to play "fast and loose." What are some of these risks?

1. They tell you only what they think you want to hear and selectively share information.
2. They omit negative information about a position or employer.
3. They put undue pressure on you to go on an interview or accept an offer.
4. They send your resume to firms with which they don't have a relationship (or the ability to present you).
5. They send your resume to an employer without your permission.

6. They obtain your permission but send your resume to firms that don't have an actual need (without prior disclosure of this fact), which results in your being rejected for the wrong reasons.
7. They engage in double blind setups (this happens on the partner side). They call one partner and say "X firm is interested in speaking with you. Would you be interested in them?" Once the partner says "Yes," the recruiter contacts the firm and says, "Partner Y is interested in speaking with you. Would you be interested in speaking with that person?" This is misleading at best and dangerously unethical at worst.
8. They lack discretion. As one partner recently shared, "One clumsy recruiter actually called my assistant to confirm I received an email regarding a change in my interview schedule."
9. They reflect poorly on you as evidenced by sloppy work product (e.g., it's not uncommon to see certain recruiters who send emails with different sized or color fonts and inconsistent formatting) or inaccurate or imprecise writing. The lack of attention to detail does not help your presentation.

As you can see from the above, your recruiter reflects you and can directly impact aspects of your lateral move. In the same manner that clients evaluate and select attorneys to assist with important legal matters, you should apply similar diligence to selecting a recruiter.

SECTION II

WORKING WITH LEGAL RECRUITERS

This section of the Guide describes how to select a recruiter (or recruiters) and maximize the relationship to create your advantage.

CHAPTER 7

YOUR RECRUITER REFLECTS YOU: PERFORMING EFFECTIVE DUE DILIGENCE ON RECRUITERS

When I was drafting this Guide I asked a close friend, a hiring partner at an AmLaw 100 firm, to review a draft. His comment was the following: *"You need to emphasize to readers that their recruiters are a reflection on them. When good attorneys decide to make a move and align with unskilled or unknown recruiters, it makes us wonder, 'What's going on here? Were they unable to get a better recruiter to represent them?'"* While it may not be fair, employers do judge candidates by the company they keep – in this case, their choice of recruiter.

In light of the above, it's alarming how few attorneys perform due diligence on their recruiters. Perhaps it's because there is so little information available that they don't know what questions to ask, or the process of making a lateral move is inherently confidential so it's hard to ask for referrals. I'm a strong proponent of carefully selecting a recruiter and understanding their pros and cons. After all, that is the intent behind this Guide.

That said, when performing due diligence on recruiters through asking them questions about their experience and preferred approach, it is important to keep in mind that your standing to perform due diligence correlates with the market demand for your skill set. If you are a partner with a $3 million+ practice or a third-year associate from Davis Polk looking for a similar law firm, ask as many questions as you would like. On the other hand, if you are a seventh-year litigation associate in a regional market, and you haven't received a call from a recruiter in two years, or if you are looking to find a recruiter who can assist you with an in-house search (as mentioned previously), this will require a more subtle approach. In other words, be realistic about your leverage to perform due diligence. If you are not in demand, some recruiters may simply decline to answer your questions.

7 IMPORTANT QUESTIONS TO CONSIDER

1. **What is the recruiter's familiarity with your practice area?** Does the recruiter understand the nature and nuances your practice area beyond a few buzzwords or acronyms? Can the recruiter effectively explain how your experience fits?

2. **Can you evaluate the recruiter in person or via video conference/ Skype?** A good recruiter will want to meet you in person, and you should strive to meet with him or her. You want to ensure your recruiter's reputation and professional or personal manner aligns with your preferences and professional approach. After all, it is rare for a client to engage an attorney to represent them in a matter when they have not met the lawyer; the same evaluation should apply to your selection of a legal recruiter.

   If an in-person meeting is not possible, it is even more critical to review the recruiter's professional background, credentials and experience, search orientation, and methodology to understand the recruiter. If a recruiter fails to present his or her own career in an effective and highly professional manner, what does this say regarding the ability to present you to employers? A happy medium could be a video conference/ Skype call at the outset so you can assess the recruiter's approach and professionalism beyond a voice and photo.

3. **Does the recruiter focus on your market exclusively or work in different markets around the country?** Staying plugged into the hiring needs in any sizable market is a full-time job. For larger markets, it takes multiple full-time recruiters to effectively stay on top of the hiring needs. A recruiter who focuses on your market — exclusively — is often informed of openings before others and may be more knowledgeable about the employers. The reason? They live, work, and have personal and professional relationships in the community in which you wish to practice. As with attorneys, there needs to be some type of specialization. An analogy is if you were a client searching for a litigator to handle a case in the Eastern District of Virginia, wouldn't you prefer to hire an attorney or firm who has handled numerous cases before the judges in that District?

    a. Exceptions:

        i. **In-house searches**: Corporations often engage recruiters working in cities where the most relevant candidates are located, even if the company is located elsewhere. For example, non-regionally based companies may engage a recruiter based in DC if there is a need for a lawyer with strong regulatory experience.

        ii. **Partner-level recruiters who are working for a particular firm**: If the recruiter has a strong relationship with a particular law firm (including the firm's leadership, which may be in multiple cities, or a practice group based in multiple regions), the recruiter's close relationship with firm leadership can be very beneficial, regardless of where the recruiter is based.

4. **How many years of experience does the recruiter have?** Interestingly, I've been asked this question only twice in my career, but the length of a recruiter's experience is something I advise every attorney to find out. To be fair, there are newer recruiters at the beginning of

their careers who often have the benefit of working with more experienced recruiters who know the ins and outs of the market. As one might expect, the new recruiter typically has a can-do, "fire in their belly" desire to make something happen for you. The newest recruiter often will need to put in more time and effort into undertaking your search than the more experienced recruiters.

Experience in recruiting is akin to experience in practicing law. Those recruiters who have been working day-in and day-out in a particular market for a long time bring significant institutional knowledge of the law firms, practices, and practitioners, which can be of great benefit to you throughout your search and career. In addition to having established relationships with key decision makers (which gives you an advantage), a seasoned recruiter has the historical experience to provide you with the access to non-published information that will help you effectively analyze which firms that are most likely to be a fit and steer you away from those that won't.

5. **When a recruiter calls, does he/she have actual experience with the employer he/she is calling about?** Just because a recruiter calls you regarding a search does not necessarily mean they have experience working with the particular firm. With online job boards and real-time subscription-based job notification services that monitor law firm websites, most recruiters find out about the publicly posted law firm openings simultaneously. This explains why on a random Wednesday afternoon when a new search is published, you may receive multiple calls within a thirty-minute period. In reality, very few of these recruiters may have been invited to work on these searches.

   Some of the recruiters calling you may just hope they "got to you first," and that you will work with them for the opening. Rather than automatically working with the recruiter who races to the phone and calls, you should specifically ask, "What is your experience with the firm?" Rather than selecting the fastest dialer, choose the recruiter who seems most knowledgeable about the particular opportunity and the firm. This information is often only obtained through prior experience with the firm, obtained through placing attorneys in the firm, speaking with attorneys over the years who were looking to leave the firm, or by having a unique personal connection to the firm.

6. **What is the recruiter's level of involvement in the process?** At times, a good recruiter literally becomes a part of your life. You may speak with your recruiter in the evenings and on the weekends. The best recruiters relish this level of involvement.

   A hands-on recruiter should do the following:

   - Spend time learning about your work history, your relevant experience, and your career goals through a personal meeting
   - Ask good and pointed questions to understand your practice and reasons for considering a move
   - Routinely notify you to available opportunities and provide insight on different employers
   - Challenge your assumptions by asking questions and offering information that contradict your assumptions about people and places
   - Provide feedback on your resume and deal sheet/representative litigation matters and/or addendum so that you present your experience in the most effective manner
   - Collaborate with you when drafting your cover letter to ensure that your narrative is communicated in the best fashion

- Present your materials to the firms in a professional manner
- Follow up on submissions and keep you updated as to their status
- Help prepare you for the interview
- Debrief with you after the interview
- Help negotiate your offer
- Support you when you're feeling anxious or uncertain about the process
- Help you with the giving-notice process
- Check in with you before you begin and after you start at your new position and be available to help with any issues that arise during integration and afterward.

7. **Did you confirm that the recruiter will never send your resume (or other identifying information) without your permission?** This is the biggest fear of most attorneys regarding working with a recruiter. It never hurts to reinforce your expectation that no action on your behalf will be initiated without your expressed authorization. To take it to another level of security, you should put authorization for each firm in writing to avoid any possible misunderstandings. The last thing you want is an overzealous and unscrupulous recruiter sending your resume around town so that he or she can "claim rights" to your candidacy. Lastly, record keeping is important. You should always maintain a written record of all the firms to which you have been submitted and the date of submission.

CHAPTER 8

ASSOCIATE VS. PARTNER RECRUITERS (AND WHAT CONSTITUTES A MORE SOPHISTICATED RECRUITER IN EACH CATEGORY)

Your experience with a recruiter will vary widely depending on whether you are seeking an associate or partner position in a law firm. Each type of search requires the recruiter to possess a fundamentally different type of skill set, and the skills of recruiters in each category can vary widely.

ASSOCIATE RECRUITERS

Overview: Associate recruiters spend time getting to know you/your practice, what you like/dislike about your current situation, your professional goals and how to find the next job that will help you achieve--or get closer to--them.

Primary contribution: Although associate recruiters assist with all stages of the process, their primary value-add is having access to, and connecting candidates with, the most appropriate opportunities as efficiently as possible. Unlike partner recruiters, who must balance the practice needs of the partner with the economic requirements of a firm, associate recruiters are focused largely on serving as a matchmaker between candidates and law firms.

What makes a mediocre vs. sophisticated associate recruiter? The below chart outlines the various stages of the associate process and highlights the differences in approaches among recruiters.

ASSOCIATE RECRUITERS		
STAGE OF THE PROCESS	**WHAT A MEDIOCRE ASSOCIATE RECRUITER DOES**	**WHAT A MORE SOPHISTICATED ASSOCIATE RECRUITER DOES**
UNDERSTANDING THE SUBSTANTIVE NATURE OF YOUR PRACTICE AND EXPERIENCE	Asks questions and takes your responses at face value with little, if any, follow-up or clarifying questions.	Asks questions but follows up for clarification, such as the breakdown of your experience (by percentages) and other important elements. You get the sense they are able to speak or write about your experience intelligently to a third person.
UNDERSTANDING WHAT IS FAVORABLE / UNFAVORABLE ABOUT YOUR CURRENT POSITION	Asks questions and takes your responses at face value with little, if any, drilling down.	Asks questions but also asks probing questions to determine whether your professional goals can be achieved internally without requiring a lateral move. May also suggest that you delay a move if your challenges are likely to be found at other firms. May ask the "hard questions" with an eye towards anticipating what law firms will ask.
UNDERSTANDING YOUR CURRENT LEVEL OF SATISFACTION AND GOALS	Asks you to explain what you are looking for in your "next job." Very little focus on long-term goals, whether personal or professional. Lack of questioning on what is going well with your current situation.	Understands both your short-term and long-term goals. Asks about your professional and personal goals, and how they will be impacted by a potential move. After the conversation, you feel that the recruiter "gets" your motivations for contemplating a move), and appreciates what is going well for you in your current firm.

ASSOCIATE RECRUITERS		
STAGE OF THE PROCESS	**WHAT A MEDIOCRE ASSOCIATE RECRUITER DOES**	**WHAT A MORE SOPHISTICATED ASSOCIATE RECRUITER DOES**
COORDINATION AND GUIDANCE REGARDING RESUME PREPARATION AND RELATED PRACTICE MATERIALS	Provides little, if any, input on the documents or how they can be improved for the particular search/opportunity.	Provides input on how to make your resume employer-friendly, which includes both substantive suggestions as well as structural and formatting recommendations, such as more effective use of headings, font changes, and other visual elements. Will also provide feedback on areas of your resume that are either unclear/should be expanded upon, or other missing elements. As to your writing sample(s) and/or deal sheet, will review and provide feedback on whether they meet industry norms or should be modified. For example, sometimes writing samples require personalized cover pages or additional levels of redactions.
DISCUSSING / INTRODUCING FIRM OPTIONS	Introduces only openings that are advertised publicly on law firm and/or and third-party websites. Information about the position is limited to the text of the job description itself, and information about the firm is limited to that which appears on the website (or third-party websites).	In addition to publicly posted openings, should have access to unpublished or exclusive searches due to established relationships with practice groups and law firms. Note: It may be helpful for you to work with a recruiter with access to research and tracking of historical hiring for certain firms, which may reflect a "soft" hiring need or trend line. These recruiters may have the ability to "create" opportunities in response to your experience and qualifications. These hidden jobs may be surfaced through marketing (often on a no-names basis) your background and experience to practice groups that the recruiter knows may be interested.

ASSOCIATE RECRUITERS		
STAGE OF THE PROCESS	**WHAT A MEDIOCRE ASSOCIATE RECRUITER DOES**	**WHAT A MORE SOPHISTICATED ASSOCIATE RECRUITER DOES**
ACKNOWLEDGING EMPLOYERS THAT DO NOT USE RECRUITERS FOR ASSOCIATE OPENINGS	Will usually avoid mentioning employers with openings that could otherwise fit your background. If they are not getting paid, they do not have an incentive to suggest you apply on your own.	Will still mention the firm as an option for you to self-apply. Although the recruiter could forgo a placement fee if you are hired, the recruiter seeks to establish a long-term relationship with you by providing the best advice. Appreciates that "what goes around comes around."
PRE-SCREENING YOUR BACKGROUND USING A BLIND PROFILE	Skips this step entirely. Alternatively, sends blind profiles to certain firms without first consulting with you, which can create uncomfortable situations (e.g., you may be conflicted from a certain firm, or may have spoken with them in the past). Or the blind profiles contain easily identifiable information (e.g., sections from your biography are lifted verbatim and can be entered into a search engine and easily associated with you).	If a particular firm (or firms) does not have a formal search but may still have a potential need/interest, the recruiter -- with your express permission -- drafts an anonymous "blind profile" (see Submissions vs. Blind Profiles: An Important Distinction). This summary explains your background in sufficient detail to enable the firm to determine if it is opportunistically interested, but is constructed in a way that protects your background from being searched/found on the Internet. If the firm expresses interest, you can authorize the recruiter to present you and reveal your identity.

ASSOCIATE RECRUITERS		
STAGE OF THE PROCESS	**WHAT A MEDIOCRE ASSOCIATE RECRUITER DOES**	**WHAT A MORE SOPHISTICATED ASSOCIATE RECRUITER DOES**
PRESENTING YOUR MATERIALS	Will send your resume, transcript, and writing sample (or deal sheet) to the firm without a personalized cover letter/profile (from the recruiter) providing key information.	Will write a detailed cover letter in addition to presenting your materials. This letter will underscore all relevant factors valued by each individual firm. It also provides other important information such as your reason for contemplating a move, explanation of prior moves, a summary of your performance evaluations/standing, and why the recruiter believes you are qualified. This process highlights your strengths and minimizes the risks of erroneous assumptions about your experience and interests.
ARRANGING INTERVIEWS	Schedules the interviews and simply asks "Do you have any questions?" before the interview.	In addition to scheduling interviews and providing in-depth details on the interviewers (when available), and will also serve as your coach by performing a "mock interview" with you to ensure you are fully prepared. The goal is to help you anticipate questions the interviewers will likely ask, and ensure you are as prepared and confident as possible.
KEEPING YOU UPDATED ON THE STATUS, INCLUDING REJECTIONS	Maintains contact when a firm is interested in an interview; does not inform you when firms decline to interview you or otherwise share negative information.	Will keep you closely updated, including when firms decline to interview. Will also attempt to learn (if possible) why certain firms passed on your candidacy.

ASSOCIATE RECRUITERS		
STAGE OF THE PROCESS	WHAT A MEDIOCRE ASSOCIATE RECRUITER DOES	WHAT A MORE SOPHISTICATED ASSOCIATE RECRUITER DOES
ONCE YOU RECEIVE AN OFFER, HELPING YOU EVALUATE WHETHER A MOVE IS JUSTIFIED IN LIGHT OF YOUR GOALS (AND, IF SO, WHICH OPPORTUNITY IS BEST)	If you are contemplating whether to stay at your current position or move (or choosing between various offers, and the recruiter is not representing you on all of them), the recruiter's advice and perspective may tend to be biased in a manner that will reward the recruiter. You may feel pressured at times.	Will listen objectively, and will help you weigh the pros and cons of each opportunity. Will have a depth of familiarity with the various moving pieces, as if the offer is his/her own. Will not "hide the ball" regarding negative information about the firm that has extended an offer (through the recruiter). Will not try to overcome your objections about the recruiter's offer. May push back on some of your assumptions, but it's for the reason of making sure you are being comprehensive in your analysis. You have a gut feeling that the recruiter wants you to make the right decision, regardless of whether it ultimately rewards the recruiter.
ANALYZING AND NEGOTIATING YOUR OFFER	Avoids negotiating the offer and expects that you will do it alone. Alternatively, may insist on negotiating it themselves which may lead to overly aggressive or clumsily stated "requirements," without benefit of a sound negotiating strategy. This may reflect poorly on you and create a negative impression with the firm.	Understands when negotiating is appropriate and when it is not. If the recruiter negotiates, he or she knows market norms and your position in them. Is skilled in analyzing the various moving pieces and provides the points of negotiation in a compelling and thoughtful manner. Never loses sight that you are negotiating with a potential future employer, and constantly preserves goodwill.

ASSOCIATE RECRUITERS		
STAGE OF THE PROCESS	WHAT A MEDIOCRE ASSOCIATE RECRUITER DOES	WHAT A MORE SOPHISTICATED ASSOCIATE RECRUITER DOES
ADVISING YOU REGARDING THE NOTICE/RESIGNATION PROCESS	Wishes you luck and asks you to call once the process is complete.	Similar to interview preparation, the recruiter prepares you for the process by helping you anticipate your firm's reaction and its likely tactics in responding to your news. The recruiter walks you through each step of the resignation process and ensures you feel prepared and "on script."
ASSISTING WITH INTEGRATION, WHEN NEEDED	You may not hear from the recruiter once you start your new job.	Stays in contact with you to ensure your integration is going smoothly, and helps you address any speed-bumps that may arise. Continues to be a resource for you.

PARTNER RECRUITERS

Overview: Like associate recruiters, partner recruiters spend time getting to know you/your practice, what you like/dislike about your current situation, your professional goals, how to find the next job that will help you achieve (or get closer) to them, and which firms may be the best options. As distinguished from associate recruiters, partner recruiters focus on finances, economics, due diligence, and the intricate process of merging practices. While associate recruiters are akin to a matchmaker knowing the landscape and setting up dates, partner recruiters delve much more into the details of what is akin to a mini-merger of sorts, even if it involves only one person.

Primary contribution: In addition to identifying which firms may provide a match (and may have an interest in your practice), they help you navigate many of the intricate aspects of the transaction on a granular level, which is often steeped in financial and practice analysis.

What makes a mediocre vs. sophisticated partner recruiter? The below chart outlines the various stages of the partner process and highlights the differences in approaches among recruiters during each stage.

PARTNER RECRUITERS		
STAGE OF THE PROCESS	**WHAT A MEDIOCRE PARTNER RECRUITER DOES**	**WHAT A MORE SOPHISTICATED PARTNER RECRUITER DOES**
UNDERSTANDING YOUR PRACTICE, INCLUDING UNDERLYING FINANCES/ ECONOMICS	Asks questions and takes your responses at face value with little, if any, follow-up or clarifying questions. Financial analysis is more superficial (e.g., "what are your portables") without further depth of analysis.	Learns not only about your experience and substantive expertise on a granular level, but the underlying finances/economics of your practice. In addition to the threshold portable business question, will also gain an understanding of billing rate structure, alternative fee arrangements, origination/ working attorney credit, necessary leverage/support from other attorneys, key clients (for conflicts), billable hours, compensation, and future business development prospects that could be impacted (positively or negatively) by a move. Will also consider your capital contributions and other back-end compensation, and how this could be impacted by the timing of a move.

PARTNER RECRUITERS		
STAGE OF THE PROCESS	**WHAT A MEDIOCRE PARTNER RECRUITER DOES**	**WHAT A MORE SOPHISTICATED PARTNER RECRUITER DOES**
UNDERSTANDING YOUR CURRENT LEVEL OF SATISFACTION AND IMPORTANT PRIORITIES	Asks you to explain what you are looking for in "your next job." Lack of questioning on what is going well with your current situation. Little focus on long-term goals, whether personal or professional.	Understands both your short-term and long-term priorities. After the conversation, you feel that the recruiter "gets" your motivations for contemplating a move (both professionally and personally). Appreciates what is going well for you in your current firm and may also suggest that you delay a move if your challenges are likely to be present at other firm. Most importantly, the recruiter understands the underlying economics of your practice.
DISCUSSING / INTRODUCING POSSIBLE FIRMS	Provides a list of firms based on more superficial factors such as whether the firm has an existing practice on its website that appears to match yours, or whether the firm's profits-per-partner are a match with your earning goals.	Provides a thoughtful analysis of why certain firms may be worth considering. Analysis goes beyond existence of similar practice areas and profits-per-partners, and also includes (when relevant) information on strategic priorities, the firm's finances, compensation structure, leadership, management philosophy, etc. In addition to discussing why certain firms may be a fit, also provides a balanced analysis on why certain proposed firms may also have shortcomings. Will not limit choices to the obvious competitor firms listed in the usual rankings, but also potential "hidden gems" that could meet your objectives.

PARTNER RECRUITERS		
STAGE OF THE PROCESS	**WHAT A MEDIOCRE PARTNER RECRUITER DOES**	**WHAT A MORE SOPHISTICATED PARTNER RECRUITER DOES**
COORDINATION AND GUIDANCE REGARDING RESUME PREPARATION AND RELATED PRACTICE MATERIALS	Offers little, if any, input on the documents themselves, or how they can be improved/enhanced for the particular search/opportunity.	If you have a resume (often optional for partner candidates), provides input on how to make it more employer-friendly. As to your business plan, will help you communicate your practice (including finances) and business goals in a way that best resonates in the lateral market.
PRE-SCREENING WHICH FIRMS MAY BE INTERESTED IN YOU BASED ON A BLIND PROFILE	Skips this step entirely. Alternatively, sends blind profiles to certain firms without first consulting with you, which can create uncomfortable situations (e.g., you may be conflicted from a certain firm or may have already spoken with them). Or the blind profiles are not crafted carefully and contain easily identifiable information (e.g., sections from your biography are lifted verbatim and can be entered into a search engine and easily associated with you).	When appropriate -- and with your express permission for each potential firm -- recruiter drafts an anonymous "blind profile" (see Submissions vs. Blind Profiles: An Important Distinction) that explains your background, financial profile, and main clients for purposes of a preliminary conflict check. This summary explains your background in sufficient detail to enable the firm to determine if it is opportunistically interested and whether there are any non-starter conflicts. It is constructed in a way that protects your background from being searched/found on the Internet. If the firm expresses interest, you can authorize the recruiter to present you and reveal your identity.

PARTNER RECRUITERS		
STAGE OF THE PROCESS	**WHAT A MEDIOCRE PARTNER RECRUITER DOES**	**WHAT A MORE SOPHISTICATED PARTNER RECRUITER DOES**
PRESENTING YOUR MATERIALS	Will send your materials to the firm without a personalized cover letter/profile (from the recruiter) providing background information.	Will write a detailed cover letter in addition to presenting your materials. This letter will underscore all relevant factors valued by each individual firm, including important financial/economic details about your practice. This letter minimizes the risks of erroneous assumptions about your practice and interests.
ARRANGING INTERVIEWS	Schedules the interviews and asks "do you have any questions?" before the interview.	In addition to scheduling interviews, recruiter will provide in-depth details on the interviewers (when available) and firm. Will also make sure you anticipate topics the firm will likely wish to explore about your practice.
FACILITATING THE INTRODUCTION OF MULTIPLE PARTNERS FROM THE SAME PRACTICE GROUP (E.G., IF YOU WOULD LIKE TO CONSIDER BRINGING OTHER PARTNERS WITH YOU TO THE NEW FIRM)	Simply presents multiple partners without fully covering issues of confidentiality.	At the outset, arranges to speak to each different potential lateral partner (from the same group) about navigating confidentiality among partners. For example, is there information (e.g., compensation details) you would prefer not to be disclosed to other partners potentially joining with you?

PARTNER RECRUITERS		
STAGE OF THE PROCESS	**WHAT A MEDIOCRE PARTNER RECRUITER DOES**	**WHAT A MORE SOPHISTICATED PARTNER RECRUITER DOES**
ASSISTING WITH THE LATERAL PARTNER QUESTIONNAIRE (AKA "LPQ")	Forwards the lengthy document and tells you to "Please complete and let me know if you have any questions."	Will help alleviate the administrative burden by filling in the information that is readily available (from your resume/biography or business plan). Will work with you closely to ensure you are interpreting certain questions consistently with industry norms, and your responses are comprehensive and accurate. At times, if certain questions are too burdensome to answer completely (e.g., asking for every matter you worked on during the past five years), recruiter can help facilitate alternative ways to respond that also satisfy the firm's needs.
FLAGS POSSIBLE ETHICAL ISSUES THAT ARISE	Will not be aware of the ethical considerations in the jurisdiction.	Will help ensure you understand, and get help if you don't, your duties and responsibilities to your existing firm. You are a partner in the firm until and through your last day at the firm. You should understand your professional/ethical responsibilities, your statutory/case law fiduciary duties to the firm and to clients, your contractual responsibilities under your partnership agreement, and other contracts/firm codes of conduct and policy. This assessment also involves what information, and in what form, may be provided to prospective new law firms.

PARTNER RECRUITERS		
STAGE OF THE PROCESS	**WHAT A MEDIOCRE PARTNER RECRUITER DOES**	**WHAT A MORE SOPHISTICATED PARTNER RECRUITER DOES**
ONCE YOU RECEIVE AN OFFER, HELPING YOU EVALUATE WHETHER IT MAKES SENSE TO MOVE (AND IF SO, WHICH OPPORTUNITY IS MOST APPROPRIATE)	If you are contemplating whether to stay at your current position or move (or choosing between various offers, and the recruiter is not representing you on all), the recruiter's advice and perspective may tend to be biased in a manner that will reward the recruiter. You may feel pressured at times.	Will listen objectively, and will help you weigh the pros and cons of each opportunity. Will have a depth of familiarity with the various moving pieces, as if the offer is his/her own. Will not "hide the ball" regarding negative information about the firm that has extended an offer (through the recruiter). Will not try to overcome your objections about the recruiter's offer. May push back on some of your assumptions, but it's for the reason of making sure you are being comprehensive in your analysis. You have a gut feeling that the recruiter wants you to make the right decision, regardless of whether it ultimately rewards the recruiter.

PARTNER RECRUITERS		
STAGE OF THE PROCESS	**WHAT A MEDIOCRE PARTNER RECRUITER DOES**	**WHAT A MORE SOPHISTICATED PARTNER RECRUITER DOES**
ANALYZING AND NEGOTIATING YOUR OFFER	Does not have a strong understanding of law firm economics or market norms for partners, and is therefore unable to advise you in a comprehensive manner. Avoids negotiating the offer and expects that you will do it alone. Alternatively, insists on negotiating it him/herself, which may lead to overly aggressive or clumsily stated "requirements," without benefit of a sound negotiating strategy.	Has a command of partner compensation structures. When appropriate/needed, is able to create spreadsheets or other similar documents to help analyze and compare compensation packages based on various moving pieces, such as capital contribution, distributions from the prior firm, and other economic or business considerations. It's particularly important that you understand, and get help if you don't, the financial consequences of your departure, the importance of timing notices of withdrawal, and whether there are times of the year that are more or less consequential. If the recruiter advises against negotiating, the rationale makes sense. If the recruiter negotiates, he or she is skilled in analyzing the many moving pieces and provides the points of negotiation in a compelling, thoughtful, and professional manner. Never loses sight that you are negotiating with a potential future partner, and constantly preserves goodwill.

PARTNER RECRUITERS		
STAGE OF THE PROCESS	WHAT A MEDIOCRE PARTNER RECRUITER DOES	WHAT A MORE SOPHISTICATED PARTNER RECRUITER DOES
ASSISTING YOU WITH PERFORMING DUE DILIGENCE ON THE FIRM, INCLUDING REVIEWING THE PARTNERSHIP AGREEMENT	May not partake in this process, due to lack of knowledge or lack of motivation to uncover possible negatives.	Will assist you with performing due diligence on the firm's finances, and help you obtain information beyond that which is publicly available. Will also assist you with reviewing the partnership agreement to draw attention to key provisions such as capital contributions, and the repayment/forfeit provisions if you leave the firm.
HELPING YOU WITH THE NOTICE/ RESIGNATION PROCESS	Wishes you luck and asks you to call once the process is complete.	Similar to interview preparation, the recruiter walks you through the process of resigning which has multiple moving pieces, including competing fiduciary duties to your current law firm and your clients. This is a complex process that can be emotional and tense, and the recruiter's experience in seeing these situations play out many times (and many ways) will help you navigate the process and maintain perspective.

General note about ethics and duties: Although lateral partners must take responsibility for their actions, and recruiters do not give legal advice, it is axiomatic that many partners are nowhere near as aware of their duties and responsibilities in some of the above areas as they should be. If your recruiter helps to ensure you are well-versed and prepared sooner rather than later, particularly regarding your ethical, fiduciary, and financial obligations, you will have a smoother process and better outcome than someone who is not.

SIDEBAR: WHAT ABOUT COUNSEL?

With counsel-level candidates, the process is often of a hybrid between associates and partners, yet differs widely depending on the nature of the candidate and situation. If a counsel candidate is being hired solely to fill an existing need for additional expertise and with little regard to business development potential, the process may be more akin to that of an associate. If the counsel candidate is being hired with an eye towards partnership and to help enhance/build a practice group (which will involve business development), the process will be more similar to that of a partner, with greater focus on financial analysis and projections.

CHAPTER 9

THE TWO RECRUITER LENSES: CANDIDATE AND EMPLOYER

Although recruiters are paid by employers, the role of a recruiter can best be described as a dual-agent — helping you, the candidate, as well as the employer. The best recruiters are able to simultaneously assist candidates with achieving their desired outcomes while also fulfilling the needs of the employer. It may be instructive to remember that the particular lens through which a recruiter views a search depends on various factors and circumstances. Although the below discussion lists two lenses recruiters can wear (candidate lens and employer lens), the purpose is to highlight for you a distinction that many candidates don't consider. It is usually not a one versus the other approach, but a blended candidate and employer orientation that facilitates the ideal outcome.

CANDIDATE LENS

Here are some characteristics of this type of orientation and the context:

- The relationship initially begins with you contacting the recruiter for information regarding lateral options.
- The recruiter may cold call you to discuss your career goals, even if the recruiter does not have a specific search he or she is calling you about; this may or may not mature into a search or a job change.

- The goal is to serve as your guide to help you navigate the lateral market most effectively.
- The recruiter takes time up front to understand your short and long-term goals and advises on a strategy to achieve your goals.
- The recruiter spends time identifying employers that may match your professional and personal goals.
- The recruiter develops list of possible options.
- With your authorization, the recruiter contacts firms on your behalf.
- The recruiter assists you with each stage of the hiring process with each firm.

EMPLOYER LENS

In this scenario, the recruiter has been asked to conduct a search on behalf of a specific firm for a specific position. Characteristics include:

- The relationship starts with the employer contacting the recruiter for help with a search, and the recruiter has extensive conversations and meetings with the employer regarding the position.
- The recruiter spends time researching and cold-calling/emailing candidates to find the perfect match.

- At the onset of the relationship, the recruiter is more invested in the needs of the employer, and how you, as a candidate, may fit into the employer's requirements.
- The recruiter will advise and help you with all steps of the process as they pertain to that employer's search.

SIDEBAR

As mentioned previously, skilled recruiters are simultaneously able to wear both lenses. For example, if a recruiter initially contacts you about a position, this does not mean they will be less responsive to your individual needs and goals. In fact, they should be equally invested in helping you with a broader search if the particular employer they are contacting you about may not be a fit, or if you wish to explore a wider range of options. At the same time, if the recruiter's interest in you is limited to how you fit into the particular search at hand (and you feel as if you are being "screened" with not much focus on your particular interests), this is a signal that the recruiter may be too near-sighted and only wearing the employer's lens.

CHAPTER 10

WHAT ARE "RECRUITER OWNERSHIP RIGHTS" OR THE 6-TO-12 MONTH SHELF-LIFE RULE?

Employers and recruiters enter into agreements that outline the terms under which a recruiter's referral will be recognized. Typically this includes authorization to refer (both your approval of that activity and the recruiter's ability to refer to that employer) as well as reflected protocols, regarding how and to whom to refer. Included in these outlines is a time period that the firm agrees to recognize a referral of a candidate from a recruiter. Here are few things to keep in mind:

- In the event two recruiters submit the same attorney to the same employer (as discussed in "The Dangers of Dual Submissions" section, this is to be avoided),), employers recognize the"first-in-time" rule to establish which recruiter has rights to your candidacy.
- **When you self-apply**: If you apply to a firm directly (i.e., without a recruiter), your recruiter won't be able to assist you with that particular firm for a period of at least six to twelve months. Because you submit yourself, or through a personal contact at the firm, you are considered a self-applicant.
  - **Example**: Let's assume you submit yourself to Employer A and within two weeks, you get rejected without an interview. One week later Recruiter B tells you that about a new position with Employer A. Recruiter B will not be able to present you to Employer A because you previously self-applied. **Possible**

exception: If Recruiter B has a close relationship with the employer, Recruiter B could place a call to the hiring authority to try to negotiate a reconsideration (and Recruiter B could then serve as your recruiter, but this is the exception).

- **When apply through a recruiter**: If a recruiter presents you to a particular employer, you will not be able to have another recruiter present you to that same firm for a period of at least six to twelve months (depending on the length of time provision in the employer's placement agreement).
  - **Example**: Let's say Recruiter A presents you to an employer and within two weeks, you get rejected without an interview. One week later Recruiter B contacts you about the same or even a different position and indicates that he or she is friendly with the firm's managing partner. If Recruiter B refers you, and you are asked to an interview, most employers would recognize Recruiter A as your recruiter due to the six to twelve-month ownership provision in the fee agreement.
  - **Risk**: Given the risk that Recruiter A and Recruiter B could have a dispute in the above situation (Recruiter B could claim that he/she was the "procuring cause" since Recruiter B's submission resulted in the interview), employers will not want to get involved in this potential conflict. If they are interested in you as a candidate, and Recruiter B is pushing back, they won't pay two placement fees but could tell Recruiter A and Recruiter B to "work it out" so that you can interview. On the other hand, as discussed, some firms may be troubled that you permitted two different recruiters to submit you (even if you had a valid reason for Recruiter B to "try again") and could simply pass on your candidacy to avoid the potential hassle, and/or because they feel that you exercised poor judgment in your search firm dealings.

- **What happens when you apply to the same firm in multiple cities**: Some firms treat each of their different offices separate and distinct for purposes of the first-in-time rule, while other view them as "all under the same roof." You want to be careful when applying to the same firm in multiple cities (as this can undermine your candidacy if not handled correctly). Your recruiter should tell you how the specific firm handles these situations and how to best navigate this.

CHAPTER 11

THE DANGERS OF DUAL SUBMISSIONS

A dual submission can occur either of two ways: (1) two different recruiters present you to the same employer within the same six or twelve month period (the particular time-frame depends on the employer's guidelines), or (2) you self-apply to an employer and a recruiter also presents you to the same employer within the six or twelve month period. **You should absolutely avoid dual submissions.**

This can adversely impact your candidacy in several ways.

- **Risk of a fee dispute**: If two different recruiters presented you, the employer will immediately become concerned that there could be a "fee dispute" between the two recruiters. A fee dispute means that two recruiters argue over who has rights to your candidacy, and the employer risks becoming entangled in the dispute. Even though the first-in-time rule applies, it can become a messy situation if the facts are unclear or disputed (e.g., one recruiter claims that the other recruiter did not have authorization, etc.). When this occurs, some employers will simply decline to interview you to avoid potential problems.
- **You appear disorganized (or over-eager/desperate)**: In addition to avoiding a fee dispute among recruiters, when two recruiters present you to the same opening, you appear disorganized. (This also occurs if you self-apply and then a recruiter subsequently presents you.) Employers infer (rightly or wrongly) that you are unable to effectively manage your search and failed to keep diligent records. Lastly, there is also

a perception that you may be a bit too over-eager to leave your current employer and therefore felt the need to work with multiple recruiters at once.

- **You exercised poor judgment and appear potentially underhanded**: As discussed later in this Guide, you are free to use multiple recruiters during your job search should you desire. But using multiple recruiters for the **same** position (or employer, within the six or twelve month period) risks portraying you in a slightly underhanded light through the eyes of the employer. At best, it reflects poor judgment. Lastly, you risk burning bridges with both recruiters as well.

Ways to avoid dual submissions:

- **Keep good records**: Keep a detailed spreadsheet of where you have been submitted, the exact date, by whom, and the status.
- **Be clear when a recruiter may (and may not) submit you**: As discussed later (in the section "How You Can Best Protect Your Interests"), there are some ways you can minimize recruiters from submitting you to an employer without your authorization (e.g., putting "DRAFT" on your resume or only authorizing submissions in writing). Although ethical recruiters will not present you to any employers without your authorization, you should know by now that there are some less ethical recruiters that are not as diligent. To be extra careful, you should make it clear to every recruiter (especially those with whom you do not have an existing relationship) that they are not authorized to speak to or approach any employer about your background without your explicit permission. You are in control and the recruiters must respect this. The good recruiters will be impressed with your level of discretion and care, and will not take it personally.

CHAPTER 12

CONFIDENTIALITY AND THE NALSC CODE OF ETHICS®

Recruiters come in all shapes and sizes, and employ various levels of judgment and discretion. You can't make assumptions at the outset. As such, it's best to explicitly ask — ideally, during your initial conversation — what type of information the recruiter will keep confidential, and what type of information will be shared with the employer(s). The parameters of what a recruiter shares with an employer should be specified by you. If in doubt, clarify what is or is not to be shared.

What must be disclosed to an employer

Employers understand that recruiters have a dual obligation to their candidates and clients. At the same time, the recruiter is prohibited from withholding essential information from the employer. The National Association of Legal Search Consultants (NALSC®), a trade association that consists of numerous recruiters in North America, has established the NALSC Code of Ethics®. This Code provides a heightened range of ethical requirements that recruiters in the Organization must abide by or be subject to disciplinary action. It states, in part, the following:

DUTIES TO CANDIDATES

- "Information provided to candidates shall be the most accurate information known to the search firm" (Article II, Relations with Candidates, §1)

- "No search firm shall withhold employer information, which a candidate would reasonably consider essential to his or her hiring decision, **subject to the search firm's duties to the employer**." (Article II, Relations with Candidates, §2) (emphasis added)

- A search firm shall treat as confidential all information supplied to it in confidence by a candidate, **subject to the search firm's duties to the employer**. (Article II, Relations with Candidates, §4) (emphasis added)

DUTIES TO EMPLOYERS

- "Information provided to employers shall be the most accurate information known to the search firm" (Article I, Relations with Employers, §1)

- "No search firm shall withhold candidate information, **which the employer would reasonably consider essential to its hiring decision**." (Article I, Relations with Employers, §2) (emphasis added)

See NALSC Code of Ethics®, *available at* http://www.nalsc.org/about/ethics.cfm (2015)

Note: Although the NALSC Code of Ethics® applies only to recruiters who are members, it is generally regarded as the heightened standard against which all recruiter activity is evaluated. Additionally, many law firms incorporate by reference NALSC's Code of Ethics in their search firm agreements regarding the duty of recruiters to disclose information that the employer would "reasonably consider essential to its hiring decision."

For this discussion, the most relevant inquiry focuses on the type of information an employer would "reasonably consider essential to its hiring decision." NALSC does not offer specific examples of this type of activity, but the following are two examples that I believe an employer would reasonably consider essential to its hiring decision:

If a candidate has been asked to leave his/her employer

- Employers expect recruiters to disclose this fact. This includes situations when an attorney remains "technically employed" (e.g., appears on the website but is winding down employment). Even if there is a perfectly justifiable, non-performance-based reason for the layoff, employers expect recruiters to disclose this outcome. A good recruiter will be experienced in handling these types of situations, will take time to understand the circumstances, and will assist you in explaining your narrative. Keep in mind that certain employers may be less receptive to paying recruiters for candidates who have been laid off (because, in their mind, they feel the recruiter fee is less justified — this is often a very incorrect assumption, but it does occur). An honest recruiter will suggest that you apply to those specific employers directly. On the other hand, the recruiter may feel that he/she can represent you and will explain your circumstances in a manner that is both truthful and helpful, and can help you overcome any negative presumptions, as explained below.
- **A true story**: A candidate informed me, in the middle of the interviewing process, that he was asked to leave his employer and had three months to find a new position. He did not want this information disclosed to the prospective employer with which he was interviewing. I insisted we disclose this development to the potential employer. After all, it would likely come out in one way or another, whether through reference checking or through due diligence questionnaires that may ask, "Have you ever been asked to leave an employer?" Additionally, the reason for the layoff — a slowdown in the relevant practice area due to market conditions — was not as negative as he believed it would be perceived, especially

since he was an otherwise strong performer. Luckily, he followed my advice. I checked references (which were very positive) and provided the firm with a detailed summary of the circumstances of his layoff as well as comments from his past performance reviews. The positive outcome was that the firm ended up hiring this associate. Had he not proactively disclosed this information, and the firm found out during the reference-checking phase, it may not have hired him due to erroneously believing that his skills were underdeveloped and/or he demonstrated poor judgment.

- You may be thinking, "What if this candidate didn't authorize you to disclose the layoff?" This has happened. In these circumstances, I strongly advise a candidate to proactively disclose this development. And, if he or she will not authorize me to do so, then I have to withdraw my representation. It's not an ideal outcome, but a match made on false or intentionally omitted information will likely be short-lived. At some point, this information is likely to surface. When it does, it will undermine your credibility and the firm's trust in you. Ultimately, it may even result in your termination for failure to disclose the prior termination.

If a candidate plans to stay at the employer for a short time (and it's not a temporary position) and is awaiting another offer

- As an example, in Washington, DC many mid-level associates wish to gain experience in the government. The government's hiring process can take a long time (for example, the background check process can take months). If a recruiter knows that a candidate regards a firm offer only as a "space filler" until a government offer is extended, the employer would regard this information as material to its decision-making process.

Accordingly, the recruiter would be obligated to disclose this information.

THE TAKEAWAYS FOR YOU TO KEEP IN MIND

- Recruiters should keep confidential information you share "in confidence." Because this is not always clear and can be a subjective classification, you should have a candid discussion with your recruiter if there is specific information you do not wish to be disclosed.
- If, at the outset, there is information about your candidacy that you do not want an employer to know because you believe it would adversely impact your candidacy — and you will not permit the recruiter to explain the situation — it is best that you apply to the employer directly.
- You should be honest with your recruiter, even regarding unfavorable information. While the recruiter owes certain duties to the employer, he or she also wants to increase your chances of getting hired. If there is a way for a recruiter to smooth certain speedbumps, you should listen to his/her advice and consider its implementation.

CHAPTER 13

SUBMISSIONS VS. PROFILES: AN IMPORTANT DISTINCTION

One of the major benefits of using a recruiter is the ability for the recruiter to test your candidacy with a particular employer without disclosing your identity. Here's an explanation of the differences between a full submission and a blind profile.

FULL SUBMISSION

- **What's shared**: Your resume, transcript, writing sample (for litigators) or deal sheet (for transactional attorneys).
- **When appropriate**: Because a full submission reveals your identity, it is only appropriate if there is either (1) an active search that matches your background, or (2) there is not an active search, but the recruiter has a reason to believe the firm would have a good faith interest in opportunistically considering someone with your experience.
- **Benefit**: The employer sees the full scope of your background and can make the most informed decision. Also, employers consider a "resume in hand" more seriously than a blind profile.
- **Drawback**: By necessity, somebody outside your firm knows your identity and that you are considering a move. That said, employers are very good about keeping your expression of interest confidential, especially when a recruiter is involved.

BLIND PROFILE

- **What's shared**: A description of your experience, year level, and other relevant information without revealing your name, current firm, or other identifying information. The recruiter shares just enough for the firm to make an initial decision on whether there is preliminary interest. If so, and subject to your consent, the recruiter can follow up with additional information such as a resume (or for partners, a biography), detailed cover letter, etc.
- **When appropriate**:
  - The employer may not have an active or known search but might be opportunistically interested in someone with your profile and prefers that the recruiter "checks first"
  - Your experience is not directly on point but could potentially be of interest to the employer
  - Confidentiality is of primary importance
- **Benefit**: It allows the recruiter to gauge an employer's interest in your profile without them knowing your identity.
- **Drawback**: Employer has more limited information to make an initial assessment and may not take the inquiry as seriously.

WHY SOME RECRUITERS AVOID BLIND PROFILES

There are some recruiters who don't utilize blind profiles because they either don't know about this approach or find the technique tedious as it requires more work for them. Instead of sending one email with your materials, the recruiter must engage in a two-step process (first sending the blind profile and, if it's a fit, revising your submission materials to include more detail about your background).

If confidentiality regarding your consideration of a move is of utmost importance, you should discuss the blind profile approach with your recruiter. In certain circumstances and depending on the employer, it is a more strategically sound way of initiating the process while minimizing your exposure risk. If your recruiter resists or does not have an informed explanation as to why this does not seem prudent, think twice about engaging this recruiter.

CHAPTER 14

HOW IMPORTANT ARE RECRUITER COVER LETTERS?

In a word, very.

If you ask a hiring attorney in a law firm what he or she considers to be the most important information (aside from academics and prior employer) when deciding to hire a lateral candidate, it's usually: (1) does this candidate have relevant experience and training to handle our work? (2) did this candidate perform well at his or her prior position?

In the world of lateral attorneys, resumes only address factor (1). You rarely see legal resumes that discuss a candidate's performance evaluations, billable hours, or reasons for leaving a prior employer. In terms of cover letters, the same problem exists when attorneys self-apply. They will typically take a paragraph to introduce their interest in the position, rehash the experience that is on their resume in a paragraph or two, and then explain in generic terms that they are "very interested" in meeting with or working for the firm.

Why is some important information not included at the outset? I don't have a good answer other than it must be rooted in tradition ("I haven't seen other people do it that way"). Or the candidates' faulty assumption that they will have the opportunity to explain the "other background information" during an interview. Unfortunately, this opportunity may not be given due to negative erroneous assumptions that frequently arise when reviewing only a resume. As one law firm recruiting manager confided,

"We tend to assume the worst unless told otherwise. We just have too many resumes to review."

THE IMPORTANCE OF A COMPREHENSIVE COVER LETTER

When working with a recruiter, you have an opportunity to have your background information presented in a compelling manner that you could not otherwise do yourself. Why? Because recruiters are speaking about you in the third-person, it is more acceptable to have them explain your background and tout relevant accomplishments through a well-crafted cover letter. An effective cover letter will not only highlight your relevant skills and experience, but will also address the precise questions the employer will formulate upon reviewing your resume, thus minimizing the likelihood of erroneous assumptions. Experienced recruiters know the types of information most relevant to a potential employer. An effective recruiter cover letter discusses not only your legal skills and experience, but any unique achievements, performance reviews, billable hours, and most importantly, your reasons for seeking another position. For example, if you are moving cities, a cover letter should explain in detail your connections/interest in the new city.

A good cover letter will not only address the questions a firm might have about your prior moves and performance history, but also can highlight why the recruiter believes you would make a good fit with the firm, based on the recruiter's knowledge of both the firm and your interests.

Additionally, given the competitiveness in the market, having a well-crafted cover letter that delivers critical information to all of the evaluating attorneys may not only help you get an interview before candidates who don't have a cover letter, but also will ensure a more productive interview.

WHAT ABOUT DISCLOSING NEGATIVE INFORMATION IN A COVER LETTER?

You may be thinking, "What if there is potentially negative information? As an associate my hours are low because my firm didn't have enough work to go around? Won't a cover letter hurt me?" Once again, I believe that appropriate, up-front disclosure is the best policy.

Getting out ahead preemptively to explain information that may arise at a later time allows you to structure the narrative. Besides, what you consider to be negative information may not be as detrimental as you might anticipate. As a reminder, even if you think you are concealing negative information going into an interview, your body language including eye contact, vocal pitch, and other cues will signal that something is not "right." As I have previously noted, it is the act of withholding information that causes the greatest damage, even if it is discovered after you are affiliated with this new firm.

With a well-crafted cover letter that accompanies your resume and transcript, you are providing potential employers with a document that contains all of your relevant background information, which is the only way to protect you from the risk of erroneous assumptions. While there is no way you can guarantee that interviewing attorneys will thoroughly prepare prior to the interview, we have found that many interviewers do read every single word of the letters (and routinely comment favorably to our candidates). If they don't read the entire letter, they usually glance at the key information that is highlighted by the effective use of headings. In sum, cover letters make the interviewer's job easier by providing relevant information at their fingertips, and this reflects well on you as a candidate.

Quite simply, a good recruiter will take the time to draft a good cover letter for and about you. Because cover letters are the vehicle through which important information is accurately and appropriate relayed, the most direct way a good recruiter can demonstrate his/her commitment and dedication to you is by taking the time to become informed about your background, interests, and fit, and reflecting that insight in the cover letter.

INHERENT RISKS WHEN YOUR RECRUITER SAYS, "DON'T WORRY ABOUT A COVER LETTER — I'LL CALL THE CONTACT AND TELL THEM YOUR INFORMATION."

When I was still a practicing attorney and worked with a recruiter, I recall asking how she was going to relay my background information to the prospective firm. She replied, "Oh, I know people at the firm. I'll just call and tell them about your additional background information." At the time, that seemed like a perfectly fine answer. What I didn't realize is that sometimes the call is never made and a resume and transcript is presented with a short email such as, "Enclosed please find the resume for ______ in connection with your _____ position." And if the call is actually made, the information that is communicated during a brief phone conversation may not be effectively distributed to all of the decision makers. The risk of erroneous assumptions presents itself again.

CHAPTER 15

WHEN TO USE ONE VS. MULTIPLE RECRUITERS

Sometimes one recruiter is quite sufficient, but in other situations, working with multiple recruiters may be best for you. The following is a chart explaining when it's most appropriate to use one or multiple recruiters.

TYPE OF EMPLOYER	YOUR GOALS	ONE OR MULTIPLE?
LAW FIRM	▪ You expect to move within the next year ▪ Recruiter acts as quarterback to find best fit ▪ Higher level of loyalty and candor	One
LAW FIRM	▪ More passive approach ▪ Will listen to positions as they arise, but no "search"	Multiple
IN-HOUSE	▪ "I want to go in-house"	Multiple (explained later in Guide)

Regardless of whether you use one or multiple recruiter, there are pros and cons to each approach.

PROS OF USING ONE RECRUITER

- Recruiter is more likely to spend time getting to know your background, strengths, and preferences
- Recruiter can serve as a quarterback to help you find the best fit vs. a more casual, scattershot approach
- Recruiter appreciates the loyalty and some may tend to prioritize your candidacy if they know you are only using them
- There is decreased risk that a second recruiter will share your materials with an identical employer, which negatively impacts your candidacy with the particular employer

DOWNSIDES OF USING A SINGLE RECRUITER

- Recruiter may not have access to all openings
- Recruiter will have stronger relationships with certain firms than with others
- You don't have much opportunity to compare different recruiter styles to determine whose approach is most complementary to yours

DO YOU HAVE TO WORK WITH THE FIRST RECRUITER WHO TELLS YOU ABOUT A POSITION?

It depends. If the recruiter has a true **exclusive search** (meaning that the recruiter has been selected by the employer as the **only** recruiter who can work on the search), then yes. The recruiter has the "keys to the kingdom." **Caveat**: On the law firm side, exclusive searches (at the associate level) are much more the exception than the norm. If a recruiter is prone to imprecise language he/she may suggest they have an exclusive by being a bit more "fast and loose" with their characterizations of the scope of their engagement with the search, if any. They may use some phrases such as "I have been retained by," or "I have been hired by ____" to give you the impression they have an exclusive search or an "in" with the law firm, when they really don't. That said, it is sometimes the case that a recruiter may have a legitimate exclusive search for a few days before the firm opens it up to additional recruiters. On the in-house side, exclusive searches are much more common.

Aside from the circumstances of an exclusive search, you don't need to work with the recruiter who first tells you about the opening if you are not comfortable with that person. Yes, it is courteous to give that person an opportunity to explain the search to you and there is a presumption that you will give that recruiter right of first refusal, but in the end you have full discretion on whether you wish to work with that recruiter for that particular employer.

Unless a search is undertaken on an exclusive basis, do not feel bullied or pressured into working with the first person who tells you about an opportunity unless you feel comfortable working with that person.

WANT TO GO IN-HOUSE? WHY YOU SHOULDN'T LIMIT YOURSELF TO WORKING WITH ONE RECRUITER

Law firms, particularly larger law firms, tend to have relationships with numerous search firms. When they open a search and post it on their website, they will accept submissions from any number of search firms (but remember, not for the same candidate). In most circumstances, whoever has the best candidate wins. This means that many recruiters can present you to the same firm; however, they may not all possess the same type of relationship with, or knowledge about, that firm.

In-house searches are different. Given how closely recruiters work with in-house clients in conducting searches, **in-house employers usually align with one search firm for each search**. So in order to fully canvass in-house opportunities, you want to speak with multiple search firms and ensure they have your resume on file in the event an opportunity opens up.

CHAPTER 16

FINDING IN-HOUSE OPENINGS AND RECRUITERS

In addition to asking for referrals from people whose judgment you value, here are the four websites I would visit to find in-house positions and/or research recruiters who focus on in-house searches:

- Association of Corporate Counsel (www.acc.com)
- GoInHouse.com
- LawJobs.com
- LinkedIn.com

After spending some time on these sites, you will notice that recruiters often provide "blind listings," which are descriptions of the positions without the employer's name. You can also gain insight into the recruiter's work quality and attention to detail by how they characterize the opportunities in the position descriptions.

APPROACHING RECRUITERS ABOUT IN-HOUSE OPPORTUNITIES

Unlike recruiters who are working on law firm positions (where they are at times seemingly begging you to consider their searches), in-house searches are the complete opposite. In-house opportunities are perceived by many as the ideal. As a result, recruiters who focus on in-house searches tend to have long lines of very qualified attorneys who wish to get on their radar. Don't be discouraged if you have a hard time speaking with a recruiter about in-house positions — they are usually inundated with calls from potential candidates.

Keep in Mind: This Guide provides numerous tips on how to perform due diligence on a recruiter, but I would be remiss if I did not provide an important distinction when it comes to in-house recruiters. To be blunt, the in-house recruiter tends to be in the driver's seat given the high demand of many attorneys for in-house openings. So unless you are a particularly in-demand candidate (e.g., corporate lawyers tend to be much more marketable for in-house positions than litigators), it may make sense to tread more carefully when performing the type of diligence you might perform on a recruiter for a law firm search (e.g., asking the recruiter about his/her experience). Why? There are certain in-house recruiters who may — wrongly, I'll add — interpret these questions as potentially insulting and could think, "Um, I have a pile of strong candidates for this position. I should be asking YOU the questions." This subtle tension is best avoided.

CHAPTER 17

CHECKLIST: HOW YOU CAN BEST PROTECT YOUR INTERESTS

- ✓ If you wish to authorize a recruiter to speak to an employer on your behalf, authorize the recruiter in writing to present you to that particular employer.
- ✓ Never provide a recruiter with "carte blanche" to "see what's out there." This is asking for unmonitored disclosure of your interests in considering another firm.
- ✓ If you send your resume to a recruiter for review but you are not ready to authorize contact with any potential future employer, type "draft resume — not for distribution" on the top.
- ✓ Don't be reluctant to ask the recruiter direct and pointed questions such as "How long have you been recruiting?" or "Have you previously placed anyone with this firm?"
- ✓ Keep a spreadsheet of where you have been submitted, by whom, and the dates.
- ✓ Make sure you have protected against dual-submissions.
- ✓ If you want a recruiter to be your search quarterback, select the recruiter like you would select a doctor for a health issue. Do research and trust your instincts.
- ✓ Consider using a recruiter who is a member of the National Association of Legal Search Consultants (NALSC) and abides by the NALSC Code of Ethics®.

CHAPTER 18

CHECKLIST: EVALUATING A POTENTIAL RECRUITER

EXPERIENCE

- ✓ Is the recruiter a referral or endorsed by someone you trust?
- ✓ How knowledgeable is the recruiter about your practice area?
- ✓ How knowledgeable is the recruiter about the market/ opportunity?
- ✓ Does the recruiter have long-standing relationships with employers in your market?
- ✓ Does the recruiter have experience working with someone with your background and interests?

APPROACH

- ✓ Does the recruiter ask questions regarding what you wish to accomplish with a move to a different employer?
- ✓ Does the recruiter focus on details, taking the time to ask questions about your interests, experience, and background?
- ✓ Does the recruiter offer market insights and suggestions regarding the structure of your search?

- ✓ Does the recruiter not only listen to your preferences but act upon those preferences?
- ✓ Does the recruiter respond to you in a prompt and comprehensive manner?
- ✓ Does the recruiter ask to meet with you, outline his or her approach, offer to review your resume and assist you with interview preparation?
- ✓ Does the recruiter hone in on questions that an employer is likely to ask and help you navigate any potential speedbumps?
- ✓ What is the quality of the recruiter's written correspondence with you (content and format)?
- ✓ How often will the recruiter keep you updated/apprised of the status?
- ✓ Will the recruiter prepare a detailed cover letter that addresses important background information regarding you and your interests?
- ✓ Is the recruiter a member of NALSC®?
- ✓ Remember, your recruiter reflects you. Choose wisely.

IN CLOSING

The goal of this Guide is to provide you with fundamental information on legal recruiters, especially as it pertains to major markets in the United States. Hopefully you now have more clarity into an often-cloudy process, and are better positioned to make smart decisions regarding legal recruiters.

As with every profession, there are good and less good among the recruiter ranks. Remember to choose wisely, and best of luck during your lateral search.

www.ingramcontent.com/pod-product-compliance
Lightning Source LLC
LaVergne TN
LVHW020236210926
848481LV00016B/2347
9780692603215